Constance Caroline Woodhill Naden

Songs and Sonnets of Springtime

Constance Caroline Woodhill Naden

Songs and Sonnets of Springtime

ISBN/EAN: 9783337007041

Printed in Europe, USA, Canada, Australia, Japan

Cover: Foto ©Thomas Meinert / pixelio.de

More available books at **www.hansebooks.com**

SONGS AND SONNETS

OF SPRINGTIME

BY

CONSTANCE C. W. NADEN

LONDON
C. KEGAN PAUL & CO., 1, PATERNOSTER SQUARE
1881

DEDICATION.

To J. C. and Caroline Woodhill.

Ye who received me, when your hearts were sore,
    With double welcome, since I came in lieu
    Of one whose fond embrace I never knew—
Your child, my mother, dear for evermore—
Who scarce had time to greet the babe she bore,
    But, dying in her spring, bequeathed to you,
    Her father and her mother, guardians true,
One little life, to tend when hers was o'er :

Ye who have watched me from my infant days
    With tenderest love and care, who treasure yet
Quaint sayings, sketches rude, and childish lays ;
Accept this wreath, entwined in April hours :
    Yours was the garden where the seed was set,
To you I dedicate the opening flowers.

CONTENTS.

THE ASTRONOMER, Etc.

	PAGE
THE ASTRONOMER	3
THE CONFESSION	11
THE ROMAN PHILOSOPHER TO CHRISTIAN PRIESTS	16
THE LAST DRUID	19
THE CARMELITE NUN	22
THE ALCHEMIST	25
THE SCULPTOR	27
THE SISTER OF MERCY	29
THE WIFE'S SONG	31
A LETTER	34
THE MYSTIC'S PRAYER	36
THE PILGRIM	39
THE PANTHEIST'S SONG OF IMMORTALITY	43
LIGHT AT EVENTIDE	46
BOOKS	48

CONTENTS.

	PAGE
MEMORY	50
LIGHT-BORN SORROWS	53
ON THE MALVERN HILLS	55
JANUARY 28TH, 1880	57
SPRINGTIDE	59
NOONDAY	61
TWILIGHT	63
YEARNING	66
CHANGED	67
SIR LANCELOT'S BRIDE	69
THE ABBOT	73
DAS IDEAL	76

THE LADY DOCTOR, ETC.

THE LADY DOCTOR	81
THE OLD LOVE-LETTERS	85
LOVE VERSUS LEARNING	88
MOONLIGHT AND GAS	91
THE TWO ARTISTS	93
MAIDEN MEDITATION	95
LAMENT OF THE CORK-CELL	98
SIX YEARS OLD	101

SONNETS.

	PAGE
JANUARY, 1879	109
TO A HYACINTH IN JANUARY	110
TO THE FIRST SNOWDROP	111
MARCH, 1878	112
MARCH, 1879	113
APRIL, 1879	114
MAY, 1879	115
STRATFORD-ON-AVON, MAY 14TH, 1880	116
IN THE LANES BETWEEN STRATFORD AND SHOTTERY, MAY 14TH, 1880	117
SUNSHINE	118
IN THE GARDEN	119
YELLOW ROSES	120
JULY, 1878	121
SUNSET	122
SEPTEMBER, 1880	123
SONGS BEFORE DAYBREAK	124
THE SEED	125
OCTOBER, 1879	126
NOVEMBER, 1878	127
DECEMBER, 1879	128
UNDISCERNED PERFECTION	129

	PAGE
THE PAINTER TO THE MUSICIAN	130
SPEECH AND SILENCE	131
BEAUTY	132
THE MYSTERY OF LIGHT	133
ILLUSIONS	134
DAY-DREAMS	135
MORNING TWILIGHT	136
SEMELE	137
THE PRIEST'S PRAYER	138
WEARINESS	139
THE AGNOSTIC'S PSALM	140
TO AMY, ON RECEIVING HER PHOTOGRAPH	141
STARLIGHT. I.	142
STARLIGHT. II.	143

TRANSLATIONS.

THE KNIGHT OF TOGGENBURG. *From the German of Schiller*	147
THE MAIDEN'S LAMENT. *From the German of Schiller*	152
THE SHARING OF EARTH. *From the German of Schiller*	154
COMFORT IN TEARS. *From the German of Goethe*	156
THE WANDERER'S NIGHT-SONG. *From the German of Goethe*	158
EVENING. *From the German of Goethe*	159

CONTENTS.

	PAGE
BURY THE DEAD THOU LOVEST. *From the German of Carl Siebel*	160
SPRING. *From the German of Ernst Schulze*	161
THE RUINED MILL. *From the German of Julius Sturm*	162
THE FIR-TREE. *From the German of Luise von Ploennies*	163
THE WELL. *From the German of Paul Heyse*	165
AN EVENING SONG. *From the German of Rückert*	167
MY ONLY ONE. *From the German of J. G. Fischer*	169
FAREWELL. *From the German of Emmanuel Geibel*	170

THE ASTRONOMER, Etc.

B

POEMS.

THE ASTRONOMER.

WHITE, cold, and sacred is my chosen home,
    A seat for gods, a mount divine;
And from the height of this eternal dome,
    Sky, sea, and earth are mine.

All these I love, but only heaven is near,
    Only the tranquil stars I know;
I see the map of earth, but never hear
    Life's tumult far below.

Bright hieroglyphs I read in heaven's book;
    But oft, with eyes too dim for these,
In half-regretful ignorance I look
    On common fields and trees.

Scant fare for wife and child the fisher gains
    From yon broad belt of lucent grey;
Rude peasants till those green and golden plains;
    Am I more wise than they?

Oh, far less glad! And yet, could I descend
    And breathe the lowland air again,
How should I find a brother or a friend
    'Mid earth-contented men?

Though, while I sat beside my household fire,
    Some dear, dear hand should clasp my own,
Must I not pine with home-sick, sharp desire
    For this my mountain throne?

I were impatient of the narrowed skies,
    Yes, even of the clasping hand;
And she, sad gazing in my restless eyes,
    Would haply understand,

And know my fevered yearning to depart,
    To dwell once more alone and free:
Well might I love, yet needs must break the heart
    That put its trust in me.

Yet hope and ecstasy desert me not,
    But coldly shine, like moonlit snows;
This earthly dream, renounced yet unforgot,
    To heavenly splendour grows.

For oft, when sleep has lulled a brain o'erwrought,
    Strange light across my brow is thrown;
The glorious incarnation of my thought,
    Urania stands alone.

She, passionless, of no fond woman born,
    Towers awful in her virgin grace;
Calmly she smiles; the first faint rose of morn
    Flushes her sovereign face.

Her atmosphere of white unswerving rays
    Athwart the fading moonlight swims;
Rare vapour, like a comet's luminous haze,
    Floats round her argent limbs.

Her clear celestial eyes look deep in mine,
    Her brow and breast gleam icy pure;
She whispers—" Be thy heart my secret shrine,
    So shall thy strength endure.

"So shall thy god-like wisdom soar above
    All rainbow hues of grief or mirth,
And I will love thee, as the stars do love
    Even thy distant earth."

Then her eyes lighten, then her voice thrills clear,
    But life and death contend in me;
And still she speaks, but now I may not hear;
    Shines, but I dare not see.

How shall immortal splendour wed the gaze
    Of man, who knows but that which seems,
Whose sight were blinded, if the sun should blaze
    With unrefracted beams?

Void were the earth and formless, if arrayed
    In purity of perfect white;
All things are clear by colour and by shade,
    Glorious with lack of light.

But what is she, whose beauty makes me blind,
    Whose voice is like the voice of Fate?
What, save a lustrous mirage of the mind,
    My slave, whom I create?

Yet from such dear illusions Wisdom springs,
    Though these may fade, she shall not die;
In fabled forms of heroes and of kings,
    E'en yet we map the sky.

Slow-conquering Truth loves well the joyous noon,
    But silent midnight gave her birth;
The cone of darkness that o'ershades the moon
    Revealed the orbëd earth.

Man knelt to constellated suns supreme,
    But as he knelt to golden clods,
Nor, till he ceased to worship, e'er could dream
    The greatness of his gods.

He wove for all the planets as they passed
    Strange legends, wrought of love and youth,
While o'er the poet-soul was vaguely cast
    A shadow of the truth.

Kinsman is he to all the stars that burn
    Mirrored in eyes of sleepless awe;
And from his brotherhood with dust, may learn
    The heavens' living law.

Nor shall the essences of Truth and Might
    Sleep ever in thick darkness furled :
Yon dim horizon bounds my present sight,
    Not the eternal world.

When the skies glitter, when the earth is cold,
    In some divine and voiceless hour,
The heavens vanish, and mine eyes behold
    The elemental Power.

Now has the breath of God my being thrilled ;
    Within, around, His word I hear :
For all the universe my heart is filled
    With love that casts out fear.

In one deep gaze to concentrate the whole
    Of that which was, is now, shall be,
To feel it like the thought of mine own soul,
    Such power is given to me.

My sight, love-strengthened, Time and Space controls ;
    No more are Force and Will at strife ;
Beyond the sun I pass ; around me rolls
    Infinite-circled Life.

This realm where he his destined orbit keeps,
　　This world of planet-ruling spheres,
Borne onward with its Pleiad-centre, sweeps
　　Through unimagined years.

In suns, that shining for some nobler race
　　Their twin-born light commingled give,
And through black depths of interstellar space
　　A boundless life I live.

To me the orbs their fiery past reveal,
　　With each minutest change designed;
Till, in this harmony of worlds, I feel
　　The future of mankind,

When each shall aid the universal plan,
　　When every deed its end shall serve,
When e'en the wildest comet-thought of man
　　Shall flash in ordered curve,

When mighty souls, that burst all prison bars,
　　Shall their diviner selves obey,
When man shall hold communion with the stars,
　　Constant and calm as they,

When every heart shall perfect peace attain,
    And every mind celestial scope;
Such were mine own, save for this hungry pain,
    This lack of earth-born hope.

I were content, though palsied, sightless, dumb,
    If, blasting toil-worn brain and eye,
The heights and depths of human joy to come
    Shone clear, before I die.

THE CONFESSION.

OH, listen, for my soul can bear no more;
    I crave not pardon; that I cannot win:
Yet hear me, Father, for I must outpour
        My tale of deadly sin.

This night I passed through dim and loathsome lairs,
    Where dwell foul wretches, that I feared to see:
Yet would to God my lot were such as theirs!
        They have not sinned like me.

And then I saw that lovely girl who stood
    Here, where I stand, some venial fault to show:
I was as fair, as innocently good,
        One long, long year ago.

High thoughts were mine, and yearnings to endure
    Some noble grief, and conquer heaven by pain:
Alas, I was a child; my prayers were pure,
        Yet were they all in vain.

Love came and stirred my breast; not fierce or vile,
   But springing stainless, like some mountain stream;
And I was happy for a little while,
      And lived as in a dream.

Thou art a priest, and dwellest far apart;
   In vain I speak of joys thou hast not known:
Even to *him* I scarce could show my heart,
      Although it was his own.

Nay, look not in my face! One night he came,
   And I sprang forward, giddy with delight:
Father! His blood-stained hands! His eyes aflame!
      His features deadly white!

Ah, wherefore ask me more? Some hated foe—
   But 'tis a common tale—thou knowest all:
A word, a gesture; then a sudden blow;
      And then—a dead man's fall.

Dumbly I heard, and could not weep or sigh;
   Gone was all power of motion, e'en of breath;
But from my heart rose up one silent cry,
      My first wild prayer for death.

"Farewell," he said, "farewell! Yet bury deep
    My bloody secret, that it shall not rise;
Or it will track and slay me, though I sleep
        Nameless, 'neath foreign skies."

Such boon he craved of me, his promised wife:
    Earth's hope, heaven's joy, for him I lost the whole:
Some give but love, and some have given life,
        But *I* gave up my soul.

"Embrace me not," I said. But ere he went
    One long impassioned kiss he gave me yet:
Still, still we loved—oh, Father, I repent—
        Would God I could forget!

Ah, not to fiery love would Christ deny
    The gift of mercy that I cannot seek:
Father, a guiltless man was doomed to die,
        And yet I did not speak.

Mine was the sin; for me it was he died,
    Slain for the murder that my Love had wrought:
How blest was he, when Death's gate opened wide,
        And Heaven appeared unsought!

But I, who dared not seek the Virgin's shrine,
    Whose very faith was madness and despair,
Lived lonely, exiled far from Love Divine,
    From peace, from hope, from prayer.

None dreamt that I consumed with secret fire,
    Nor knew the sin that withered up my youth:
I wasted with a passionate desire
    Only to tell the truth.

But now they say that he I love is dead;
    Calmly I listen; see, my cheeks are dry;
My heart is palsied, all my tears are shed;
    And yet I would not die.

Let me do penances to save his soul,
    And pray thy God to lay the guilt on me;
Strong is my spirit; I can bear the whole,
    If that will set him free.

For could my expiating woe and shame
    Raise him to Paradise, with Christ to dwell,
Then were there joy in purgatorial flame—
    Nay, there were Heaven in Hell.

And then, perchance, when countless years are past,
  Ages of torment in some fiery sea,
The grace of God may reach to me at last;
    Yes, even unto me.

THE ROMAN PHILOSOPHER TO CHRISTIAN PRIESTS.

WELL have ye spoken, but the words ye said
    Stir in my constant soul nor love, nor rage ;
Through you my life is bare, my joy is dead,
    Yet speak I calmly, as a Roman sage.

Behold the myriad orbs, whose light from far
    Darts through the spherëd heavens, when day is done :
What if the dwellers in yon faintest star
    Deem its weak light more glorious than the sun ?

And were it granted those dim eyes to share
    The glow of noon that glads our earth and sea,
Would they not hate the white unpitying glare,
    And choose to dream in starlight, e'en as ye ?

Clear truth to vulgar minds no comfort yields;
    The fair old myths have served their purpose well:
Is Heaven more bright than our Elysian fields?
    And was not Tartarus sufficient Hell?

Till now, the ancient symbols have sufficed;
    But there is room for all; the world is wide:
Zeno was great, and so, perchance, was Christ,
    And so were Plato, and a score beside.

If I were young, I might adore with you;
    But knowledge calms the heart, and clears the eye:
A thousand faiths there are, but none is true,
    And I am weary, and shall shortly die.

It is not rest, to stand for evermore
    And chant with myriads round a flaming throne;
I crave not this your heaven; my life is o'er,
    And I would slumber, silent and alone.

Ye cannot give me back my one desire:
    How have ye changed my daughter, my delight!
Since I, forsooth, must writhe in quenchless fire,
    While she sings anthems, clad in vestal white!

I have not warred with doctrines, but with deeds;
    In fair and generous mood I met you first;
I hated not her teachers, nor their creeds,
    And yet she scorns me as a thing accursed.

She deems my lordly house unclean, defiled;
    She scarce will sip my wine, or taste my bread.
Ye boast of virgin martyrs—if my child
    Die for her faith, my vengeance on your head!

Ye sons of slaves, unworthy to be free!
    Calmly I speak, yet fear me, crafty priests!
I will arouse the people—they shall see
    Your bodies hacked with knives, or torn by beasts.

Go, eat and drink, and call your feast divine;
    But, if my daughter dies, ye shall not live:
The ancient Roman spirit still is mine,
    And I forget not, neither can forgive.

THE LAST DRUID.

Despairing and alone,
Where mountain winds make moan,
   My days are spent:
Each sacred wood and cave
Is a forgotten grave
   Where none lament.

This is my native sod,
But to a stranger God
   My people pray;
Till to myself I seem
A scarce remembered dream
   When morn is gray.

I know not what I seek;
My heart is cold and weak,
   My eyes are dim:

Across the vale I hear
An anthem glad and clear,
   The Christians' hymn.

Oh, Christ, to whom they sing,
Thou art not yet the King
   Of this wild spot;
I am too weary now
At new-made shrines to bow;
   I know Thee not.

They say, when death is o'er
Man lives for evermore
   In heaven or hell;
They call Thee Love and Light:
Alas! they may be right,
   I cannot tell.

But if in truth Thou live,
If to mankind Thou give
   Life, motion, breath;
If Love and Light Thou be,
No longer torture me,
   But grant me death.

Give me not heaven, but rest;
In earth's all-sheltering breast
   Hide me from scorn:
The gods I served are slain;
My life is lived in vain;
   Why was I born?

Gone is the ancient race;
Earth has not any place
   For such as I:
Nothing is true but grief;
I have outlived belief,
   Then let me die.

These dim, deserted skies,
To aged heart and eyes
   No comfort give:
Woe to my hoary head!
Woe! for the gods are dead,
   And yet I live.

THE CARMELITE NUN.

Silence is mine, and everlasting peace;
   My heart is empty, waiting for its Lord;
All hope, all passion, all desire shall cease,
   And loss of self shall be my last reward.

For I would lose my life, my thought, my will;
   The love and hate, the grief and joy of earth:
I watch and pray, and am for ever still;
   So shall I find the death, which yet is birth.

Yet once I loved to hear the wild birds sing,
   I knew the hedge-row blossoms all by name;
Keen sight was mine, to trace the budding spring,
   Clear voice, for songs of joy when summer came.

Too dear I held each earthly sight and sound,
   Too well I loved each fair created thing,
And when I prayed to Him I had not found,
   I called Him in my heart "the mountains' King."

All, all is past—gone, every vain delight;
    No beauty tempts me in this lonely cell:
Yet why, O Lord, were earth and sky so bright,
    Winning the soul that in Thyself should dwell?

Often my heart recalls the sacred time
    When fell the tresses of my nut-brown hair;
But then will come—O God, forgive the crime!—
    That guilty question—Can I still be fair?

I cannot quite forget that I am young;
    I sometimes long to see my mother's face:
Oh, when I left her, how she wept, and clung
    About my neck in agonized embrace!

And there was one—Ah, no, the thought is sin—
    Why come these thronging forms of earthly grace?
Close, close, my heart! Thou shalt not let them in,
    To break the stillness of this holy place.

Oh, Mary, Mother! help me to endure!
    I am a woman, with a heart like thine:
But no—thy nature is too high and pure,
    Thou canst not feel these low-born pangs of mine.

Oh, for the vision of the Master's face !
    Oh, for the music of the heavenly throng !
I have but lived on earth a little space,
    And yet I cry, " How long, O Lord, how long ? "

THE ALCHEMIST.

In lonely toil my manhood has been spent,
    Spurning all ties of home, all joyance free;
And now my heart is sick, my frame is bent,
    And I would sleep, but rest is not for me.

Two gifts I seek, two wondrous powers unknown
    Shall yield their treasures to my dauntless mind;
The meaner, boundless wealth to me alone;
    The nobler, endless life for all mankind.

My star of distant hope doth far transcend
    All dew-drop glories, that around me lie:
With Nature I will struggle to the end;
    Conquer I must, though conquering I should die.

Though I should die, ere I have tasted life,
    Losing the heritage I give to all;
Though, as I grasp the trophy of the strife,
    My battle-wearied arm should powerless fall.

I conquer still, though strength may not be mine
    To drink the cup my dying hand prepares;
My life, but not my triumph I resign,
    For all mankind shall be my deathless heirs.

I care not who the victor's crown may wear,
    I care not, though my bones neglected lie:
This is my latest, this my only prayer—
    Come life, come death, let not my wisdom die.

Yet oh! sweet Life, for whom I long have served,
    Whose glorious beauty I from far have seen,
Not this reward thy votary deserved,
    Not this thy warrior's guerdon should have been.

Oh no, it cannot be! for I shall live,
    And priceless bounty royally impart,
And life and love, and wealth and gladness give,
    Dug from the treasure caverns of my heart.

I still will hope, and struggle for the crown;
    Night shall not come, before I grasp the truth;
For I will yet behold my just renown,
    And feel at last the fresh delight of youth.

THE SCULPTOR.

Before the noblest form his genius wrought
    The sculptor stood : with awe, but not with pride,
He saw the image of his highest thought,
    His inner self, transfigured, purified.

He spoke with sad emotion, half concealed,
    Like one who sorrows, but would fain rejoice ;
No glad content was in his eye revealed,
    Nor any thought of triumph in his voice.

" This is my grand ideal. 'Twas for this
    I gave my strength, while yet an eager boy ;
Leaving fresh mirth for some diviner bliss,
    Trusting to Hope my fair estate of joy.

" But Hope is gone for ever. I am left
    With this sublime fulfilment of my dreams ;
Not of the midnight loveliness bereft,
    Yet clear and steadfast in the noonday beams.

"Oh, that some charm were wanting! that some stain
    Marred the ideal grace my vision wore!
For I may live, but cannot hope again,
    And I may toil, but shall advance no more.

" I saw my rival frown, his cheek turn pale,
    In envy of the fame so dearly bought;
But this I know—the hope of those who fail
    Is better than the victory they sought.

" Yet in my heart some new delights may spring,
    As humble flowers on lordly ruins live;
Still shall my work some tranquil pleasures bring
    Though not the ecstasy it once could give.

" I do not grieve that glowing youth is spent,
    Nor would I quench the yet remaining fire;
Since lofty joy dwells not with calm content,
    Nor peaceful happiness with strong desire."

THE SISTER OF MERCY.

SPEAK not of passion, for my heart is tired,
I should but grieve thee with unheeding ears;
Speak not of hope, nor flash thy soul inspired
In haggard eyes, that do but shine with tears.
Think not I weep because my task is o'er;
This is but weakness—I must rest to-day:
Nay, let me bid farewell and go my way,
Then shall I soon be patient as before.
Yes, thou art grateful, that I nursed thee well;
This is not love, for love comes swift and free:
Yet might I long with one so kind to dwell,
Cared for, as in thy need I cared for thee:
And sometimes, when at night beside thy bed
I sat, and held thy hand, or bathed thy head,
And heard the wild delirious words, and knew
Even by these, how brave thou wert and true,
Almost I loved—but many valiant men
These hands have tended, and shall tend again;
And now thou art not fevered or distressed

I hold thee nothing dearer than the rest.
Nay, tell me not thy strong young heart will break
If to thy prayer such cold response I make;
It will not break—hearts cannot break, I know,
Or this weak heart had broken long ago.
Ah no! I would not love thee, if I could;
And when I cry, in some rebellious mood,
" To live for others is to live alone;
Oh, for a love that is not gratitude,
Oh, for a little joy that is my own!"
Then shall I think of thee, and shall be strong,
Knowing thee noblest, best, yet undesired:
Ah, for what other, by what passion fired,
Could I desert my life-work, loved so long?
I marvel grief like thine can move me still,
Who have seen death, and worse than death, ere now—
Nay, look not glad, rise up; thou shalt not bow
Thy knee, as if these tears thy hope fulfil:
Farewell! I am not bound by any vow;
This is the voice of mine own steadfast will.

THE WIFE'S SONG.

I. NIGHT.

SHE kneels with folded hands, as though she prayed;
  Over her pure, pale cheek the moonlight streams,
And o'er the slender form, in white arrayed;
  Her room is consecrate to bridal dreams,
And she is like some lonely priestess-maid,
  Believing, though her god be silent long,
  And in his temple chanting secret song.

" To heaven I lift my longing eyes,
    Knowing that yonder tranquil moon
  Is bright for you in western skies.
    And has she power your soul to tune
  In subtlest harmony divine
  With all the passioned thoughts of mine?

"Nay, rather let her give you rest,
    In peace to sleep, with joy to wake;

Yet, if a dream the slumber break,
Dream of my yearning lips and breast,
Hungered and lone, far off and sad,
But dream them near, and dream them glad!"

II. Morning.

Now has she slept; nor fell there any blight
    Over her beauty from those wakeful hours;
Her darkest grief was but a moonlit night,
    Tuneful with birds, and sweet with summer flowers,
Closed by an early daybreak of delight;
    And now she lifts anew her matin chant,
    With all the garden choir conjubilant.

"The morning sunshine floods my room,
    Its tender glow my brow has kissed,
And scattered all the night-born gloom;
    Yon, floating, thin, translucent mist,
Pierced through and through with living gold
    Makes lovelier what it half enshrouds,
And you in distant skies behold
    The self-same sun, but other clouds.

"Trim English lowlands bloom for me,
    For you, Atlantic waves are bright;
For both, o'er earth, and sky, and sea,
    Through thought and passion, mind and heart,
    Still streams the same all-glorious light:
Earth's barriers keep us far apart,
    But we are one at heaven's height."

A LETTER.

Only a woman's letter, brown with age,
   Yet breathing deathless love, too strong and deep
E'er to be told, save by the written page,
   That cannot blush, or hesitate, or weep :
Only a letter, treasured by the dead;
   Voiceful, yet ever powerless to impart
   Its hidden melodies to any heart
Alien from hers who wrote, from his who read ;
Save as a lute long silent, waked at last
   By heedless fingers, or by winds that thrill
   The chords untuned, may feebly murmur still
Some love-sweet echoes from the tuneful past.

Take my one treasure : take, and ever keep
   My whole heart's love : nor shall the gift be vain,
   Although it cannot bring you rest from pain,
Nor glad forgetfulness, nor tranquil sleep.

Oh, that my power were boundless as my love!
   Then would I give to him I hold so dear
   Joys faintly dreamt by many an ancient seer,
Chanting sweet fables of the heavens above.

" Alas," I thought, " such dreams are all too bright,
Too poor am I, of god-like gifts to sing;"
   But you have said, that even these I bring;
You tell me, that to raptured touch and sight,
   I seem the essence of ethereal Spring,
The incarnation of perfume and light.
Wherefore I will not grieve, but gladly twine
   Amid your mellow fruit my virgin flowers :
   All have their time for love, and this is ours;
Let us rejoice, while yet the sun doth shine.

THE MYSTIC'S PRAYER.

My God, who art the God of loneliness,
    Who, Life of human souls, art yet alone,
Who, Lord of joy, dost bear the world's distress,
    Come Thou, and quench my being in Thine own;
    Come, in this mute cathedral make Thy throne
While moonlight through the blazoned window streams,
    Where kings and saints a ceaseless vigil keep;
Their reflex glories, like celestial dreams,
    Haunt the grey carven brows of those who sleep,
    Illuming changeless eyes, that will not wake and weep.

Thy sleep, O Christ, hath sanctified their calm;
    Their hands point upward; yet nor wish nor care
Doth move Thy tranquil souls to join the psalm
    Sung in this ancient home of tears and prayer.
Yes, these are dead; but I, who live and breathe,
Would learn of them, and dying would bequeath

A memory of one, who deaf to sound
Communed with Silence, guardian of all truth;
  Who, with divinest midnight compassed round,
  The secret soul of earth and heaven found,
And knew the heart of Death, wherein are life and
    youth.

For this one hope I wrestle, day and night;
  In this one faith I joined thy chosen saints,
And left my virgin love, my young delight,
An earth-born cloud, that seemed most fair and white
  Until I looked beyond, and saw the sun,
And blinded by his beams, desired not sight.
  Now might I dream that heaven is almost won,
Save that yon pale Madonna's plaintive smile
  Thrills me with anguish, till my spirit faints,
Till, even in this lone cathedral aisle,
  A sad voice murmurs—" Didst thou scorn thy life
For love of God? and hath He sealed thy choice?
  A maid contented, or a happy wife
I might have been." Hush, Lord, this bitter voice.
  I am not worthy, save of Thy disdain,
Yet unto Thee have I performed my vow,
  And tortured soul and sense, and prayed for pain;

It cannot be that Thou wilt scorn me now,
    That Thou hast let me toil and agonize in vain.

Not martyrdom I crave, nor length of days;
But grant me, Lord, ere this frail form decays,
    The perfect union that my soul has sought,
The ecstasy that knows nor prayer nor praise,
    The raptured silence, unprofaned by thought.
No more wilt Thou in heavenly dreams appear,
    When of Thy mystic Essence I am part,
For mine own soul I see not, nor can hear
    Even the pulsings of this fevered heart,
Fevered and weary; but full calm is near;
Almighty calm, in endless being blest,
Infinitude of life, too deep for aught save rest.

THE PILGRIM.

There was a land, where all men lived in dreams,
    Where heaven was hid by vapours, grey or gold ;
Yet real seemed their life, as our life seems,
    And lovers wooed, and merchants bought and sold ;
But e'en mid feast, and song, and soft caress,
Each heart was sore with utter weariness.

And some were rich, some miserably poor,
    And each for other felt a dull contempt ;
And some were fools, of loftiest wisdom sure,
    And some seemed wise, but no man knew he dreamt ;
If any woke, men shrank with angry fear,
Or smiling said, "What doth this dreamer here?"

But at the last, one minstrel boy awoke,
    And strove to rouse his fellows, but in vain ;

Till, strong and flushed with hope, away he broke,
    And left them revelling in mirthful pain :
His hands were trembling from a last embrace,
Yet somewhat sternly smiled the youthful face.

His golden singing-robes were cast aside,
    The roses all were shed, that wreathed his brow;
No more 'mid guilty dreams might he abide,
    Who in his heart had sworn a solemn vow
To find the ancient innocence again
In some far land, unknown of weary men.

No kindred nature deemed his purpose good;
    The vision and the promise were his own :
High hills he climbed; through many a tangled wood
    He cut his way, in darkness and alone,
Or built a trembling bridge where wild waves tossed,
Or in a fragile boat the surges crossed.

On sandy plains he saw fair miraged lakes,
    And oft he hungered, and was oft athirst;
Through haunts of savage beasts and venomed snakes
    He roamed, still bravest when the path was worst;

Toiling for heedless kinsfolk unforgot,
For those delirious hearts, that knew him not.

But when he next shall speak, they *must* awake ;
   Or if this last best triumph may not be,
Yet will he struggle, e'en for life's dear sake—
   What lustre blinds him ? Has he strength to see
That primal Heaven on Earth, desired so long,
Won with no joy-burst, greeted with no song?

Oh, glorious recompense for vanished youth,
   For love untasted, for the silenced lyre !
This is indeed that ancient land of truth,
   Nobler than thought, more lovely than desire :
The snow-crowned heights are girt with blossoms sweet,
And grass lies cool beneath his fevered feet.

But is there respite here for soul and flesh ?
   Are yonder glades but homes of idle calm ?
This is no dreamland—here the wind blows fresh,
   Lulling the sense with no voluptuous balm ;
Full life inspires the pilgrim's heart and eyes
From yon bright waves, yon high unclouded skies.

Shall he not twine fresh garlands for his head,
    And seek new singing-robes of quaint device?
Here roses blush, more delicately red
    Than e'er he dreamed the flowers of Paradise,
And in this lovely land is plenteous store
Of gems and gold, more rich than once he wore.

Ah no! Exulting 'neath yon radiant sky
    For youth's forgotten songs he oft may yearn;
But the unflinching hand, the wakeful eye,
    Still tireless to their lonely task shall turn:
Ere his limbs fail, ere his strong heart be dumb,
Let him make plain the path, that all may come.

THE PANTHEIST'S SONG OF IMMORTALITY.

Bring snow-white lilies, pallid heart-flushed roses,
    Enwreathe her brow with heavy-scented flowers;
In soft undreaming sleep her head reposes,
    While, unregretted, pass the sunlit hours.

Few sorrows did she know—and all are over;
    A thousand joys—but they are all forgot:
Her life was one fair dream of friend and lover;
    And were they false—ah, well, she knows it not.

Look in her face, and lose thy dread of dying;
    Weep not, that rest will come, that toil will cease:
Is it not well, to lie as she is lying,
    In utter silence, and in perfect peace?

Canst thou repine, that sentient days are numbered?
    Death is unconscious Life, that waits for birth:
So didst thou live, while yet thine embryo slumbered,
    Senseless, unbreathing, e'en as heaven and earth.

Then shrink no more from Death, though Life be gladness,
    Nor seek him, restless in thy lonely pain :
The law of joy ordains each hour of sadness,
    And firm or frail, thou canst not live in vain.

What though thy name by no sad lips be spoken,
    And no fond heart shall keep thy memory green ?
Thou yet shalt leave thine own enduring token,
    For earth is not as though thou ne'er hadst been.

See yon broad current, hasting to the ocean,
    Its ripples glorious in the western red :
Each wavelet passes, trackless; yet its motion
    Has changed for evermore the river bed.

Ah, wherefore weep, although the form and fashion
    Of what thou seemest, fades like sunset flame ?
The uncreated Source of toil and passion,
    Through everlasting change abides the same.

Yes, thou shalt die : but these almighty forces,
    That meet to form thee, live for evermore :
They hold the suns in their eternal courses,
    And shape the tiny sand-grains on the shore.

Be calmly glad, thine own true kindred seeing
    In fire and storm, in flowers with dew impearled;
Rejoice in thine imperishable being,
    One with the Essence of the boundless world.

LIGHT AT EVENTIDE.

Evil has brought forth good, but good in turn
Brings evil forth, and painfully we learn
    The rich resulting harmony of life :
Triumphant glories, that most brightly burn,
    Last not the longest ; for the worth of strife
Consists not in the crown the victors earn.

The man who truly strives can never fail ;
    For though at set of sun
    The battle is not won,
And he is left, despairing and alone ;
Yet through the gloom, when flesh and spirit quail,
    New radiance flashes, e'en to hope unknown.

He that can walk in darkness, will not slip
    Although some bright surprise
    At first may blind his eyes ;
The ancient glow comes back to heart and lip,
    And tears remembered make his laughter wise.

Fresh love and joy, not seeking, he shall find,
    While Truth at last her promised garland weaves,
Not of gay roses or green laurels twined,
    But bright with scarlet berries, amber leaves.

In some fair glade he seems awhile to rest,
    All Dead Sea fruits forgot;
  Wild songsters chant, wild breezes blow;
His path is overgrown, his brow caressed
    By blossoms, that he did not sow,
      And foliage, that he tended not.

And what though once, in vain yet noble quest,
    With burning feet and eyeballs dim,
  He strove to scale volcanic heights of power?
    Since on the fertile terrace grew for him
Wisdom and Love, rich fruit and glorious flower.

BOOKS.

Oh, fatal fruits, nurtured with tears and blood!
To taste your richness, we have given youth,
Unshadowed mirth, and calm credulity;
Your heavy perfume spoils the wild-flower scent
Wafted around us by the winds of heaven.
Ye steal the young delight, that was so sweet,
The simple, thoughtless joy in all things fair,
Giving instead a weary questioning,
A striving for what cannot be attained,
A cloudy vision of the inner life.
We might have lingered in our paradise,
Hearing no music sadder than the notes
Of dreamy birds; while Hope and Memory,
Still young and fair and gaily innocent,
Still undefiled by any touch of doubt,
Together trod the dewy meads of life.

Thus said I, in unreasoning complaint,
Bitterly railing on the friends I love .

Because their voice and sweet companionship
Must bring the grief that ever comes with joy.
My heart was full: each common sight and sound
Seemed fraught with mournful meaning; and the earth
Was like a hopeless bride, bedecked in vain
With gems and flowers, for one who will not come.
What wonder I rebelled against the art
That taught me thus to think in metaphors,
And gave me reasons for my soul's unrest?
For I remembered not that it had drawn
My higher nature forth, and given voice
To secret melody. I missed the truth
That knowledge is a greater thing than mirth,
And aspiration more than happiness.

MEMORY.

Precious glimpses through the future's curtain
    He may catch, who sees the past unveiled ;
Else, in seeking for a goal uncertain,
    Blindly groping, will and heart had failed.

What were love, its faded flowers uncherished?
    What were life, its bygone days forgot?
Memory may live, when hope has perished :
    Hope were dead, if we remembered not.

All our past, in colours soft and tender,
    Stretches backward, till it melts in night ;
While the future, robed in hazy splendour,
    Shows us transient phantoms of delight ;

Glorified reflections of the present;
    Spirits of the days that once have been ;
Hopes of bright perfection, when life's crescent
    Fills the orbëd outline, dimly seen.

Yesterday's delights will haunt to-morrow,
   Subtle essences of vanished joys,
Till the spectre of remembered sorrow
   Their ethereal witchery destroys.

Rays of memory have sunned our pleasure ;
   In the self-same light regret will spring :
Sorrow is man's burden, yet his treasure,
   Proves him servant, yet proclaims him king.

Sharpest anguish, meaner things besetting,
   Finds a perfect and a swift relief :
Man alone, immortal, unforgetting
   Wears the sombre coronal of grief.

In his heart a quenchless fire is burning,
   Kindled ere his conscious life began :
Lord of restless thought and noble yearning
   Reigns in loneliness the soul of man.

Yet the earth must yield him free communion,
   Heights of heaven his daring hope must gain,
Till he joy in that eternal union
   Which the struggling spirit may attain.

Linking Past, and Present, and Hereafter
   Man shall find a staff, where seems a rod :
Solemn memories, that check his laughter,
   Draw him nearer to the heart of God.

LIGHT-BORN SORROWS.

Hath Wisdom made thee weep? Be yet more wise,
And sing for joy. The blind man, gaining sight,
Says haply, "Would I ne'er had seen the light!
This world is all so strange, my 'wildered eyes
Know nought of fair or foul : ah, dear content,
Ere any spectre came to me at night,
When, watched and soothed by unimagined skies,
My dreams were nought but music and sweet scent.
Now must I link to faithful touch and tone
A wondrous alien form, unloved, unknown,
And try to read the face that may be sweet
When I have learnt its language—not till then.
E'en if I shut my eyes, am blind again,
And strive, undoubting, that dear voice to greet,
To trust the hand, that still must guide my feet,
The phantom that I know not comes between ;
I must look up—I, who was blind from birth,
And conning wistfully her face and mien,

Interpret mystic features by clear voice,
Loving the song, must love the plumage too,
And make the rose's scent explain its hue :
Thus, keeping faith in beauty, I rejoice,
(Or hope for joy) in green fields, heavens blue,
In all my new-found plenty, felt as dearth,
In all enigmas of this visible earth."

Ah, think ye not, if that poor man be wise,
He will exult because his night is past,
Saying " Although it come to baffled eyes,
Yet light is good, and shall be sweet at last :
From this new face, that even now grows dear,
I shall but learn more richly cadenced love,
And all this foreign world, around, above,
Shall float like music to my inward ear ;
Amid all discords, through all thunder-strife,
My soul shall glory in perfected life."

ON THE MALVERN HILLS.

In pleasant shade I walk, while sunshine lies
   On many a distant slope,
And far above me, gold-green summits rise,
   Like steadfast towers of Hope.

My hands are full of wreathèd bryony,
   And bracken from the hill;
And sated with the beauty that I see
   My very heart is still.

Lonely I step o'er this elastic sod;
   All living things are dumb;
But whispering of heights I have not trod
   The mountain breezes come.

Only a little while my heart can rest,
   A little while forget
The rugged paths to many a sun-lit crest
   That must be mounted yet.

Take, wild fresh winds, my fading flowers and fern;
    These joys I may not keep:
Sweet slumberous glade, farewell! When I return,
    It will be time for sleep.

JANUARY 28TH, 1880.

No more I long for April's fitful sheen,
    For little fluttering lives, that passed in June,
        For leaves and flowers, by sad October lost ;
Since now in ecstasy mine eyes have seen
    The rich blue heaven of a summer noon
        O'er dazzling trees, thick-robed with mossy frost.

Amid the leafless hedge-rows jewel-twined,
    Great trunks and boughs, not crystal-clad as they,
        Like black majestic arches I behold ;
All wreathed and crowned with woven sprays, defined
    In every tender shade of pearly grey,
        And radiant white, that glitters into gold.

Around the mighty limbs all gnarled and bowed,
    The oak-tree twigs are finely interlaced ;
        The willows droop in bright cascades of foam,
Each distant tree, a white and feathery cloud,
    The nearer branches, delicately traced,
        And gleaming pure against the azure dome.

JANUARY 28, 1880.

The winds are hushed—there comes no murmuring
    breeze
  To stir the poplar's lofty sun-lit cone,
    Or myriad branchlets of the wide-spread beech :
Through this all-glorious temple of the trees,
  As through the house of God, I walk alone ;
  A silence, as of worship, is their speech.

SPRINGTIDE.

The silver birch, with pure-green flickering leaves,
Flooded by morn with golden light, rejoices,
And mingles with the kindred merriment
Of perfume-laden winds and happy voices:
No child of spring is lonely, but receives
Some subtle charm, by diverse beauty lent,
And with another life its own inweaves;
E'en man's creative eyes win all their gain
From light, whose glory, but for him, were vain.
While bud the flowers, while May-tide sunshine beams,
Through all the world of mind and body streams
One constant rapture of melodious thought,
One fragrant joy, with summer promise fraught,
And one eternal love illumes the whole;
For odour, light, and sound are truthful dreams,
Inspired by Nature in the human soul.
This fresh young life, whereof my own is part,
With boundless hope all earth and heaven fills;

The birds are waking music in my heart,
A voiceless chant, more sweet than they can sing;
My thoughts are sunbeams; all my being thrills
With that exultant joy whose name is Spring.

NOONDAY.

The deep enchantment of the summer-tide
    Lay o'er the earth, and hill and valley dreamed,
And all the trees with light were glorified,
    That through the half-transparent foliage gleamed.

The sunbeams brightly pierced the deep-red beech,
    Kindling the sombre leaves to scarlet flame:
Like half-articulate, melodious speech,
    The thousand murmurs of the noonday came.

All sounds were mingled in one dreamy tune;
    All joys were fused in one supreme delight:
No hope, no fear, profaned that lustrous noon,
    Nor any dim forebodings of the night.

It was a poet's paradise of rest,
    Where, for a season, heart and brain might sleep:
Not now by passion and by thought possessed,
    Yet ripening golden grain, that they must reap.

Grain to be harvested with anxious toil,
    Winnowed and crushed, till fullest worth be won :
But first, in light and heat, the fruitful soil
    Receives the inspiration of the sun.

And even night, with depth of mystic gloom,
    And even Autumn, with its slow decay,
Bring no more solemn message than the bloom
    And joyful splendour of a summer day.

To each grand thought, some beauteous form replies ;
    The soul, exalted to its noblest height,
Grows like the pure, illimitable skies,
    The chosen home of Mystery and Light.

TWILIGHT.

The radiant colours in the west are paling;
    Fast fades the gold, and green, and crimson light,
And softly comes, each trivial object veiling,
    The all-ennobling mystery of night.

This is the hour of thought and silent musing,
    When poets' fancies tender buds unfold;
Like the sweet primrose of the twilight, choosing
    To spend on evening noonday's gift of gold.

These blossoms hide within their deep recesses
    Treasures the wandering wind can never seize;
Not all its inner wealth the flower confesses,
    Nor gives its choicest perfume to the breeze.

What wizard's wand can charm the secret sweetness
    From the fair prison, where it lies concealed?
What poet's lay can show in grand completeness
    The inmost heart, by human speech revealed?

We twine the spell of rich harmonious numbers,
    We conjure up the graceful words in vain :
Our lighter fancies waken from their slumbers ;
    Without a voice the noblest thoughts remain.

So dash the restless billows of the ocean,
    But bring no tidings of the tranquil deep ;
Above, are endless tumult and commotion ;
    Below, are silence and eternal sleep.

Beneath the realms that human skill discloses,
    Where Life and Death have ceased their ancient fight,
The deep foundation of the earth reposes,
    A temple sacred to primæval night.

In wild rejoicing, and in vengeful madness,
    Men haste o'er vale and mountain, sea and shore,
But calmly, underneath their grief and gladness,
    The earth's great secret lies for evermore.

Above, the sky with myriad stars is gleaming ;
    Fair in their light the sleeping land appears ;
And yet that radiance, o'er the earth down-streaming,
    Tells not the wonders of the distant spheres.

And far beyond the realms of starlight glory
    Are mysteries too high for Fancy's wing,
Nameless alike in science and in story,
    In all that sage can tell or poet sing.

As height and depth alike transcends our vision,
    The human soul whence clearest lustre beams,
Has yet its Hades and its fields Elysian,
    Revealed alone in symbols and in dreams.

For there are griefs, that none has ever spoken,
    Joys, that no mortal tongue has power to tell;
The silence of the soul must be unbroken,
    Till to the speech of earth we bid farewell.

YEARNING.

I murmur songs of past delight,
    To tunes of present pain :
Around me is the empty night
    That answers not again.

My thoughts were better told by tears,
    And yet I scorn to weep :
Forgetting hopes, forgetting fears,
    My eyes and heart shall sleep.

Yet must I see, in visions wild,
    The joys I cannot gain,
And like a little lonely child,
    Stretch out my arms in vain.

CHANGED.

They told me she was still the same,
   In form, and mind, and heart;
With freshly-dawning joy I came,
   And now in grief depart.

Still round the forehead, smooth and white,
   The golden tresses twine,
The face is fair, the step is light,
   As when I called her mine.

And yet the mouth that once I kissed
   Is not the same as then;
The smile of love I never missed
   Comes not for me again.

More measured is the silver voice,
   The words more fitly said;
But while she speaks, I half rejoice
   To feel my love is dead.

The eyes are deeper than before,
    And far more subtly sweet;
And yet I pray that mine no more
    Their altered glance may meet.

My dream is past. I loved a child,
    The woman I resign;
The world and she are reconciled,
    And now she is not mine.

SIR LANCELOT'S BRIDE.

Soft blows the breeze, the sun shines bright,
    The birds sing loud and gay;
But from the castle on the height
    Sounds forth a blither lay.

The hall is decked with flowerets fair,
    The gates are opened wide,
To welcome home that youthful pair,
    Sir Lancelot and his bride.

The lingering hours pass slowly by,
    The blossoms droop and fade;
And many a bright impatient eye
    Looks down the rocky glade.

"Look forth, my son, adown the height,"
    Outspeaks a harper old;
"Methought I saw a helmet bright
    Flash back the sunset's gold."

"Sir Lancelot's band draw nigh, my sire,
    Their hundred helmets gleam,
And like a line of living fire
    They ford the shallow stream.

"Hurrah! hurrah! they come, they come!
    But why so slow and sad?
Why march they not to beat of drum,
    With shouts and laughter glad?

"Oh, sweet and sad their music streams,
    In cadence low and long;
More like a funeral dirge it seems,
    Than a gay bridal song."

"Look forth again," the old man said,
    "Thy sight is strong and clear;
What bear they on that narrow bed,
    That looks so like a bier?"

"I see the gleam of golden hair,
    As slowly on they ride:
For weird in beauty, strangely fair,
    They bring Sir Lancelot's bride.

"They bear her through the rocky dale;
   Methinks they sigh and weep:
My lady's cheek is deadly pale—
   Oh, say, can that be *sleep ?*

"She lies in all her loveliness,
   A fair yet awful sight;
And that is not her bridal dress,
   That gleams so ghastly white.

"The light falls on her lily cheek,
   And on her golden head—
Oh, hush, or but in whispers speak:
   Say not—that she is dead!

"Alas, alas! in deep despair
   Sir Lancelot's head is bowed:
He hides his face; he cannot bear
   To see the snow-white shroud."

Within the hall the flowerets fair
   Ere now have drooped and died;
Fit welcome to that mournful pair,
   Sir Lancelot and his bride.

The morn shall come with brighter flowers,
　　The lark shall warble gay;
But never more shall Lancelot's towers
　　Send forth a gladsome lay.

THE ABBOT.

Slowly, with dream-like sadness, tolled
    The monastery bell;
The Abbot of those cloisters old
    Lay dead within his cell.

The monks were gathered round his bed;
    Solemn and still they stood;
The fearful presence of the dead
    Awed that stern brotherhood.

They gazed upon his hoary head,
    And on his noble brow;
They saw the form whence life had fled—
    Where was the *spirit* now?

Strong will was his, a nature stern,
    That loved nor wine nor gold:
Did youthful passion ever burn
    Within that bosom cold?

The monks had loosed his rugged vest,
    While yet alive he lay :
What saw they on that wasted breast
    That gleamed so golden gay ?

No shining cross, no image fair,
    Those eager brethren found ;
Only a tress of golden hair,
    With a black ribbon bound.

They gazed upon that witness dumb,
    That told of love and death ;
Some spake with scorn, with pity some,
    But all with bated breath.

" Lay it again upon his breast,"
    An ancient brother said ;
" His soul hath entered into rest ;
    Judge not the silent dead.

" Long hath he lived a life apart
    From every earthly snare ;
Yet who shall say what aching heart
    Throbbed 'neath his shirt of hair ?

"Blame not his long-enduring love,
  Nor call it weak and vain,
But pray that he, in realms above,
  May meet his bride again."

They buried him beneath the shade
  Of cloisters grey and old ;
And near his silent heart they laid
  That treasured lock of gold.

DAS IDEAL.

"Denn sehet, das Reich Gottes ist inwendig in euch."
Luc. xvii. 21.

Meinem verehrten Freunde Herrn Dr. Lewins in
Dankbarkeit gewidmet.

Ich bin ein Sonnenkind, und strebe immer
    Hinauf zum ew'gen Licht;
Der Erdentag, der enge Wolkenschimmer
    Stillt meine Sehnsucht nicht.

Genügt es mir, auf Bergeshöh' zu wohnen,
    Der scheuen Gemse gleich?
Nein! wo kein Adler schwebte, muss ich thronen,
    Wie in der Ahnherrn Reich.

Zerreissen will ich die geträumten Schleier
    Des Stoffs, des Raums, der Zeit,
Und mich ergiessen, frei und immer freier,
    In die Unendlichkeit.

DAS IDEAL.

Nie soll es mir an Brudergeistern fehlen,
  Wie hier im Lügenrauch;
Das todte Weltall will ich selbst beseelen,
  Mit leichtem Gotteshauch.

Der Wind verstärkt sich nur durch eignes Wehen,
  Die That gebiert die Kraft:
Ich *bin* noch nicht. Erst kann der Mensch entstehen,
  Wenn er als Gott erschafft.

Umsonst! Was hilft's, dass sich der Wahrheit Funkeln
  Zu vollem Tag vermehrt?
Selbst auf dem Sonnenthron muss sich verdunkeln
  Das Herz, das stets begehrt.

Wie sollt' ich laben mein verdurstet Wesen
  Mit leerem, schwankem Schein?
Nur an der Erde Brust kann ich genesen
  Von scharfer Himmelspein.

Verzeih' mir, o Natur, das kind'sche Lallen,
  Den rasenden Gesang:
Doch was bist *Du*, als nur das Wiederhallen
  Vom alten Seelenklang?

Der kühne Dichtertraum ist nicht verloren,
    Er war zu eng, zu bleich:
Nur in des Menschen Seele wird geboren
    Das Erd- und Himmelreich.

THE LADY DOCTOR, Etc.

THE LADY DOCTOR.

Saw ye that spinster gaunt and grey,
Whose aspect stern might well dismay
   A bombardier stout-hearted?
The golden hair, the blooming face,
And all a maiden's tender grace
   Long, long from her have parted.

A Doctor she—her sole delight
To order draughts as black as night,
   Powders, and pills, and lotions;
Her very glance might cast a spell
Transmuting Sherry and Moselle
   To chill and acrid potions.

Yet if some rash presumptuous man
Her early life should dare to scan
   Strange things he might discover;
For in the bloom of sweet seventeen
She wandered through the meadows green
   To meet a boyish lover.

She did not give him Jesuit's bark,
To brighten up his vital spark,
   Nor ipecacuanha,
Nor chlorodyne, nor camomile,
But blushing looks, and many a smile,
   And kisses sweet as manna.

But ah! the maiden's heart grew cold,
Perhaps she thought the youth too bold,
   Perhaps his views had shocked her;
In anger, scorn, caprice, or pride,
She left her old companion's side
   To be a Lady Doctor.

She threw away the faded flowers,
Gathered amid the woodland bowers,
   Her lover's parting token:
If suffering bodies we relieve,
What need for wounded souls to grieve?
   Why mourn, though hearts be broken?

She cared not, though with frequent moan
He wandered through the woods alone
   Dreaming of past affection:

THE LADY DOCTOR.

She valued at the lowest price
Men neither patients for advice
   Nor subjects for dissection.

She studied hard for her degree;
At length the coveted M.D.
   Was to her name appended;
Joy to that Doctor, young and fair,
With rosy cheeks and golden hair,
   Learning with beauty blended.

Diseases man can scarce endure
A lady's glance may quickly cure,
   E'en though the pains be chronic;
Where'er that maiden bright was seen
Her eye surpassed the best quinine,
   Her smile became a tonic.

But soon, too soon, the hand of care
Sprinkled with snow her golden hair,
   Her face grew worn and jaded;
Forgotten was each maiden wile,
She scarce remembered how to smile,
   Her roses all were faded.

And now, she looks so grim and stern,
We wonder any heart could burn
   For one so uninviting;
No gentle sympathy she shows,
She seems a man in woman's clothes,
   All female graces slighting.

Yet blame her not, for she has known
The woe of living all alone,
   In friendless, dreary sadness;
She longs for what she once disdained,
And sighs to think she might have gained
   A home of love and gladness.

Moral.

Fair maid, if thine unfettered heart
Yearn for some busy, toilsome part,
   Let that engross thee only;
But oh! if bound by love's light chain,
Leave not thy fond and faithful swain
   Disconsolate and lonely.

THE OLD LOVE-LETTERS.

To-day I've discovered a treasure
   Tied up with a ribbon of blue;
That record of pain and of pleasure,
   A packet of old billets-doux.

The note-paper, quite out of fashion,
   The date of ten summers ago,
Recall the unreasoning passion
   Of juvenile rapture and woe.

No face was so lovely as Minnie's,
   I praised it in prose and in verse;
Her curls were like piles of new guineas—
   Alas, she had none in her purse!

I loved her for beauty and kindness,
   I grieved when I fancied her cold,
But Cupid, quite cured of his blindness,
   Now takes a good aim at the *gold*.

To fair Lady Flora, the heiress,
    I've offered my love and my life;
Repenting of ancient vagaries,
    I'll settle to wealth and a wife.

The heat of my boyhood is banished
    Alike from my heart and my head;
The comet for ever has vanished,
    But fireworks will answer instead.

I've kept all my ardent effusions,
    Appeal, protestation, and vow:
I'm cured of my youthful delusions,
    And can't write such love-letters now.

The thing was excessively silly,
    But then we were only eighteen,
And she was all rose-bud and lily,
    And I was uncommonly green.

I'm happy to say she was fickle,
    She blighted my love with a frown;
It withered, ere Time with his sickle
    Could cut the first blossoming down.

THE OLD LOVE-LETTERS.

We parted—how well I remember
   That gloomy yet fortunate day!
It seemed like the ghost of December,
   Aroused by the frolics of May.

I shook myself loose from her fetters—
   (I did not express it so *then*);
'Twas well she returned me the letters,
   For now I can use them again.

I am not afraid of detection,
   I cast all my scruples away;
The embers of former affection
   Shall kindle the fire of to-day.

LOVE *VERSUS* LEARNING.

Alas, for the blight of my fancies!
   Alas, for the fall of my pride!
I planned, in my girlish romances,
   To be a philosopher's bride.

I pictured him learned and witty,
   The sage and the lover combined,
Not scorning to say I was pretty,
   Nor only adoring my *mind*.

No elderly, spectacled Mentor,
   But one who would worship and woo;
Perhaps I might take an inventor,
   Or even a poet would do.

And tender and gay and well-favoured,
   My fate overtook me at last:
I saw, and I heard, and I wavered,
   I smiled, and my freedom was past.

LOVE VERSUS LEARNING.

He promised to love me for ever,
   He pleaded, and what could I say?
I thought he must surely be clever,
   For he is an Oxford M.A.

But now, I begin to discover
   My visions are fatally marred;
Perfection itself as a lover,
   He's neither a sage nor a bard.

He's mastered the usual knowledge,
   And says it's a terrible bore;
He formed his opinions at college,
   Then why should he think any more?

My logic he sets at defiance,
   Declares that my Latin's no use,
And when I begin to talk Science
   He calls me a dear little goose.

He says that my lips are too rosy
   To speak in a language that's dead,
And all that is dismal and prosy
   Should fly from so sunny a head.

He scoffs at each grave occupation,
    Turns everything off with a pun;
And says that his sole calculation
    Is how to make two into one.

He says Mathematics may vary,
    Geometry cease to be true,
But scorning the slightest vagary
    He still will continue to woo.

He says that the sun may stop action,
    But he will not swerve from his course;
For love is his law of attraction,
    A smile his centripetal force.

His levity's truly terrific,
    And often I think we must part,
But compliments so scientific
    Recapture my fluttering heart.

Yet sometimes 'tis very confusing,
    This conflict of love and of lore—
But hark! I must cease from my musing,
    For that is his knock at the door!

MOONLIGHT AND GAS.

THE poet in theory worships the moon,
    But how can he linger, to gaze on her light?
With proof-sheets and copy the table is strewn,
    A poem lies there, to be finished to-night.
He silently watches the queen of the sky,
    But orbs more prosaic must dawn for him soon—
The gas must be lighted; he turns with a sigh,
    Lets down his venetians and shuts out the moon.

"This is but a symbol," he sadly exclaims,
    "Heaven's glory must yield to the lustre of earth;
More golden, less distant, less pure are the flames
    That shine for the world over sorrow and mirth.
When Wisdom sublime sheds her beams o'er the night,
    I turn with a sigh from the coveted boon,
And choosing instead a more practical light
    Let down my venetians and shut out the moon."

He sits to his desk and he mutters "Alas,
   My Muse will not waken, and yet I must write!"
But great is Diana: venetians and gas
   Have not been sufficient to banish her quite.
She peeps through the blinds and is bright as before,
   He smiles and he blesses the hint opportune,
And feels he can still, when his labour is o'er,
   Draw up his venetians and welcome the moon.

THE TWO ARTISTS.

"Edith is fair," the painter said,
    "Her cheek so richly glows,
My palette ne'er could match the red
    Of that pure damask rose.

"Perchance, the evening rain-drops light,
    Soft sprinkling from above,
Have caught the sunset's colour bright,
    And borne it to my love.

"In distant regions I must seek
    For tints before unknown,
Ere I can paint the brilliant cheek
    That blooms for me alone."

All this his little sister heard,
    Who frolicked by his side;
To check such theories absurd,
    That gay young sprite replied:

"Oh, I can tell you where to get
    That pretty crimson bloom,
For in a bottle it is set
    In Cousin Edith's room.

"I'm sure that I could find the place,
    If you want some to keep;
I watched her put it on her face—
    She didn't see me peep!

"So nicely she laid on the pink,
    As well as *you* could do,
And really, I almost think
    She is an artist, too."

The maddened painter tore his hair,
    And vowed he ne'er would wed,
And never since, to maiden fair,
    A tender word has said.

Bright ruby cheeks, and skin of pearl,
    He knows a shower may spoil,
And when he wants a blooming girl
    Paints one himself in oil.

MAIDEN MEDITATION.

"I'll don my kerchief blue," she said,
   "And wear my Sunday gown,
For every morn, with lightsome tread
   A youth goes by to town.

"And ever as he passes by,
   Methinks he walks more slow,
And glances up, with wistful eye,
   To where I sit and sew.

"And sometimes, with a tender sound
   He whistles soft and low;
How can that gentle youth have found
   That I love music so?

"His flashing eyes reveal his soul,
   They are so very bright;
And ever in his button-hole
   He sticks a lily white.

"He never dons a flaunting rose,
  But always wears the same;
Perhaps it is because he knows
  That Lily is *my* name!

"I'll wear a wreath of lilies white
  Methinks, when I'm a bride—
Oh, here he comes, with footstep light—
  But—who walks at his side?

"It's some one in a scarlet shawl;
  Perhaps *he* calls her fair,
But *I* don't think she's nice at all:
  I hate that yellow hair!

"How *can* he walk with such a fright?
  Oh dear, what *shall* I do?
He's given her that blossom white!
  Is *her* name Lily too?

"But now I look at him, he seems
  Less handsome than before;
His eyes have lost their radiant gleams,
  His voice is sweet no more.

"His hair, methinks, is getting red,
  His nose less straight appears:
I could not such a creature wed,
  Though he should sue for years!

"And other youths for me may sigh,
  And I may love again,
But never, never more will I
  Watch at the window-pane!"

LAMENT OF THE CORK-CELL.*

FAREWELL, oh mocking Wind! No more I mix
    Thine airy substance with my world, the Tree:
Farewell, oh Carbon, that I cannot fix,
    And Oxygen, that I no more set free!

They tell me I have helped the trunk to grow,
    The roots to suck the earth, the boughs to fork,
The fruits to ripen—well, it may be so,
    But I am dying, and shall soon be cork.

Dead, sapless cork! yet I remember still
    My moist and merry life in windy March;
How green I was! how full of chlorophyll!
    But soon it shrivelled, leaving only starch.

---

* Towards the end of summer, the cells immediately beneath the epidermis of a young shoot usually become converted into cork. Their green colour is changed to brown, and the walls are rendered almost impervious to water, so that vital functions are no longer possible.

LAMENT OF THE CORK-CELL.

Blest epoch! when transparent and elastic,
    My membrane scarce restrained its endoplast,
When, homogeneous, semi-fluid, plastic,
    My vital molecules rotated fast.

Dry as I am, I once was young and tender,
    Alive with chemic yearnings; then, alas!
What thoughtless joy was mine, in spring-tide splendour,
    To decompose carbonic acid gas!

Oh, had I sunk to inorganic slumber,
    And left the atoms to their gaseous glee!
The greatest pleasure of the greatest number
    My life may serve—but what is that to me?

Backward I look, as o'er a fearful chasm
    To days when I rejoiced to live and grow;
Now less and less becomes my protoplasm,
    My nucleus divided long ago.

My wall grows thicker, dryer—oh to issue
    From this dark prison, where compressed I dwell,
To live, no more a part of any tissue,
    But a primordial protoplasmic cell!

A cell amœboid, drifting from its mother,
    Naked and houseless in the cruel storm,
Having no aid of sister or of brother,
    Nor any cellulose to keep it warm;

Yet having freedom! Nay, the dream I banish,
    The time of cell-division long is past;
Slowly and surely, all my contents vanish,
    My walls are waterproof—I'm cork at last!

SIX YEARS OLD.

THEY'VE left me alone in the garden,
  So I'll talk to that dear little wren—
Mr. Beetle! I *do* beg your pardon,
  I was very near killing you, then.

I'll tell you a tale, Mrs. Robin,
  Please do not be frightened at all—
A tale about Neddy and Dobbin—
  She's gone! she's flown over the wall!

That wall must be *very* old—maybe
  They're the children of Israel's bricks;
It was built before I was a baby,
  And now—only think—I am six!

Six years old! What a beautiful swallow,
  Catching flies! How I wish he could speak!
He's gone down to that house in the hollow;
  I went there to dinner last week.

I could stay in that garden for ever,
   And make friends with the beeches and limes:
I saw Dr. Jones—he's *so* clever;
   He writes to the papers, sometimes!

He looked at me hard through his glasses,
   And said, " Now make plenty of noise,
Have a regular romp with my lasses,
   And be petted and teased by the boys."

He said that my curls wanted rumpling,
   My cheeks should be red and not pink,
He called me a sweet little dumpling—
   He's very insulting, I think.

'Twas Nurse that had made me so tidy,
   And how can I help being small?
He gave me some roses on Friday;
   Perhaps he is nice, after all.

I stayed with the children till seven;
   They're kind, but so dreadfully rough!
There were ten of them—I made eleven—
   We played Tick, French and English, and Buff.

SIX YEARS OLD.

The girls are as bad as their brothers,
   They teased me, and played me such tricks!
But Maude isn't rude like the others,
   She says I look older than six.

She showed me her dog and her kittens,
   And the birds, and the fish in the pool:
She crochets her scarves and her mittens,
   And goes to Miss Trimmington's school.

She mustn't make blunders or stammer,
   Or stoop when she sits on the bench;
She knows History, Science, and Grammar,
   Geography, Tables, and French.

She takes pepper and mustard at dinner,
   She may ask for plum-pudding again:
I wish I were taller and thinner,
   I wish—how I *wish*—I were ten!

She has brothers and sisters—a dozen—
   And Rover, and Pussy, and Poll;
But I haven't even a cousin,
   I've only Mamma, and my doll.

Papa's out all day in the City,
  And I'm often in bed when he comes;
He's so tired and so grave—what a pity!
  When *will* he have finished his sums?

I wish there were more of us, only
  It's nice to play just what I please;
And when I am mopish and lonely
  I always can talk to the trees.

Mamma says, "Sweet flowers will not tarry,
  But trees are companions for life."
I wish that great lime-tree could marry,
  With me for his dear little wife!

Sometimes, when I shoot at the sparrows
  (I don't want to hit them, they know),
I peel his small twigs for my arrows,
  And bend a strong branch for my bow.

If he died, oh, how much I should miss him!
  (It's only his *dry* sticks I peel)
I put my arms round him and kiss him,
  And sometimes I think he can feel.

Those beautiful green caterpillars
  Live here, that Nurse cannot endure ;
And the birds—cruel butterfly-killers !
  But they don't know it's wrong, I am sure.

I make tales about flying and creeping,
  About branches, and berries, and flowers ;
And at night, when I ought to be sleeping,
  I wake and lie thinking for hours.

I keep quiet, that Nurse may not scold me,
  And think, while the stars twinkle bright,
Of the tales that Aunt Mary has told me,
  And wonder—who comes here at night?

I fancy the fairies make merry,
  With thorns for their knives and their forks,
They have currants for bottles of sherry,
  And the little brown heads are the corks.

A leaf makes the tent they sit under,
  Their ball-room's a white lily-cup :
Shall I know all about them, I wonder,
  For certain, when I am grown up?

Far over the seas and the mountains
   There's a wonderful country of light;
My new home—full of castles and fountains;
   My Dolly goes there every night.

I've seen it in dreams—there are plenty
   Of birds and beasts, talking in verse;
I shall take Mamma there when I'm twenty,
   And Papa, and Aunt Mary, and Nurse.

Papa will look glad, when I show him
   Such new and such beautiful things;
He'll be pleased when I write my grand poem,
   And paint a bright angel with wings.

I'll swim, with a mermaid and merman,
   Through the seas and the ocean so broad,
I'll learn French, and Italian, and German,
   And soon be as clever as Maude.

I'll often have tea at Aunt Mary's,
   With marmalade—orange and quince:
I'll visit the queen of the fairies,
   And then I will marry a prince!

SONNETS.

JANUARY, 1879.

With bounding heart, with eyes and cheeks aglow,
   Not caring how the frost may stab and sting,
   I haste along, where leafless branches fling
Their clear blue shadows o'er the sun-lit snow.
For though I count sad Winter as my foe,
   Within my heart I can create the Spring,
   Can hear sweet music, ere the thrushes sing,
And see white flowers, before the pear-buds blow.

These homely scenes, whence first my childish eye
   Its own ideal form of beauty chose,
I love for ever; leaves and blossoms die,
But this ethereal image lingers yet;
   And if I grieved, I could but grieve for those
Who know not Spring, or having known, forget.

TO A HYACINTH IN JANUARY.

Sweet household hyacinth, whose dainty breath
   Steals through my spirit like an April dream!
   Each day I watch another snowy gleam,
That dawns and brightens through thine emerald
   sheath:
The encircling air, the water from beneath,
   The fireside glow, the pallid noon-day beam,
   Arise transfigured in thy white raceme,
Safe from the New Year's wind, whose touch were
   death.

The bells of Spring are not so sweet and fair,
   For they with wind and rain and hail must cope,
     That all too soon their tender life destroy;
But thou, warm sheltered from the frosty air,
   Art like some delicate and hidden hope,
     More full and fragrant than the promised joy.

TO THE FIRST SNOWDROP.

FAIR, sunny-hearted child of many tears!
   Thou, while thy mother Earth forsaken slept,
   Didst gather to thyself pure hopes, that crept
Through stormy dreams; and now the sun appears,
White buds reflect each rare faint smile, that cheers
   The home where thine unshapen germ was kept,
   Safe in deep midnight, while the heavens wept,
Or hung the shuddering trees with frosty spears.

Now springs to life and light each buried joy,
   With broken music and with tearful glow,
With drooping blossoms, winter-pale and coy;
For Love shall soon fulfil her long desire—
   Her face and breast are memories of snow,
Her heart, like thine, is lit with vestal fire.

MARCH, 1878.

THE blackbird sits and pipes his love-notes clear
   In yon dark tracery of budding sprays,
   Sharply defined against the distant haze,
But soon 'mid fresh green leaves to disappear:
Now soft, now keen, the wind breathes hope and fear,
   While with unsheltered almond flowers it plays:
   The skies are sad, remembering winter days,
But birds and blossoms know that Spring is here.

I, too, foresee her glory, and rejoice;
   Though to my heart she comes in wintry guise,
Dark-robed, slow-stepping; for in eye and voice
Are promises of music and of light,
   And I can wait till smiles shall come for sighs,
And golden hues for grey, and bloom for blight.

MARCH, 1879.

Ye little birds, that chant your love so loud,
    Your careless hearts are not so glad as mine,
    For he who sings because the sun doth shine,
Is robbed of joy by every murky cloud;
And ye, sweet heralds of the summer crowd
    Of unremembered flowers, whose tints combine
    To light the meadows—ye grow pale and pine,
When by cold winds your radiant heads are bowed.

From you, from all fair creatures of the earth,
    I do but gain the beauty that I give;
Your form, your music, in my soul have birth,
    And in my very life your colours live;
    And when the sunlight fades, and ye depart.
    I hold your joy within my secret heart

APRIL, 1879.

Clear, golden, soft, the spring-tide sunshine beams,
    With tranquil splendour piercing grove and dingle,
    As though bright morning, noon and, eve, could mingle
In some eternal home of daylight dreams;
    Even as though this radiance were not fleeting,
    But shone for ever from the slumbering skies,
    Calming with tender light impassioned eyes,
And sleepless brain, and heart too strongly beating.

Yet cold March winds prepared these breezes warm,
    And heralded this glow of April weather,
    And soon dim flakes of cloud will float together,
Till earth be sad once more with rain and storm;
    For all fresh glory must be born of strife,
    And still perfection were but death in life.

MAY, 1879.

At last, coy Spring, concede one festal day
    To us who yearn thy beauty to behold;
    These pallid leaves, that peer above the mould,
Perfume and brighten; lanes and woods array
With hawthorn, that was wont to bloom in May,
    White-petalled, crimson-anthered; lilies cold,
    With drooping bells that hide their central gold,
And sun-bright buttercups, and cowslips gay.

Long have we listened to a song of death,
    That wild winds chant o'er living seeds entombed:
Sing thou of life; inspire us with thy breath;
Transfuse thy lustre e'en through clouds and showers;
    Our hearts shall glow, like dells by thee illumed,
    Whose shadows are but images of flowers.

STRATFORD-ON-AVON, MAY 14TH, 1880.

THE grey old church is solemn in the sheen
    Of noonday—half its reverend beauty won
    From that blind, silent, lifeless denizen
Who sleeps within; whose living soul is seen
In tall and arching lindens, freshly green,
    With light leaves golden-twinkling in the sun;
    In all sweet May-tide joyance, new begun,
That sings or blooms where frost and snow have been;
    And in the rippling, daisy-bordered river,
That flashes back the joy of God and man,
    And whispers to fresh hearts, that wake and quiver,
Such melodies, as round young Shakespeare wove
    Their spells, while near his feet the Avon ran,
Changeful, yet changeless, e'en as life and love.

IN THE LANES BETWEEN STRATFORD AND SHOTTERY, MAY 14TH, 1880.

Through dreamful meads, that still his spirit keep,
    Roamed the boy-poet, when the morn was young,
    And listened while the skylark's mirth out-rung,
Though his own heart was warbling strains more deep;
And 'mid half-wakened king-cups, thought of sleep
    More sweet than theirs, that waited till he sung,
    And bade it flee; then to his eyes there sprung
Such gladsome tears, as waking, she might weep.

Here with his Love he wandered to and fro,
    Yet 'mid his utmost passion of desire,
High hopes, deep thoughts, had room to live and grow;
Here, while he mused of old heroic strife,
    His blood leapt through his veins, a fount of fire,
And all his nature glowed with boundless life.

SUNSHINE.

Come, tender sunlight of the spring, and shine
    Through all my thoughts; my inmost being fill,
    Teaching my heart to glow, and yet be still,
With that victorious quiet which is thine.
Oh that my hand had cunning to combine
    The tints wherewith thou robest copse and hill!
    But I, so rich in love, am poor in skill,
d praise fair Truth, yet may not build her shrine.

But every spirit, worshipping aright,
    Must glory in the gifts that others bring;
    So would I triumph—not as one apart,
But with the kindred throng who love the light,
    Joying in beauty that transcends my art,
    And mutely dreaming notes I cannot sing.

IN THE GARDEN.

Sweet sounds, and scents, and colours join to woo
    My musing heart to love and reverence;
    A tender and a subtle influence
Comes from each graceful form, each brilliant hue;
Strange power have they, my spirit to imbue
    With thoughts above themselves; for e'en while sense
    Adores the Beautiful with joy intense,
The soul, far gazing, only seeks the True.

And ye, fair flowers, translating to my sight,
    In gold or blue the pure uncoloured beams,
Are poets and revealers of the light;
Soon is your message told, your life-work done,
    For all your tints are only passing dreams
Of the eternal splendour of the sun.

YELLOW ROSES.

My sweet sun-tinted roses, faint and fair
    As morning twilight! though ye soon must fade,
    Still shall ye bloom for me. I will not braid
Soft leaves and fragile blossoms in my hair,
But for a few bright hours, with loving care
    I strive to paint the golden light and shade
    Wherein each curling petal is arrayed,
And the translucent green your leaf-sprays wear.

So would I keep sweet hopes, that else might die,
    And fragrant fancies, withering too fast,
All fresh delight in earth, and sea, and sky,
And the deep joy, so near akin to grief;
    That from the slumberous garden of the past
I may not lose one sun-reflecting leaf.

JULY, 1878.

Like waves that rise and fall, the morning sheen
   Glows between quivering leaves, which fain would
     fling
   Their dust and blight to breezes, murmuring
Sweet May-time legends 'mid the sombre green.
Alas for wistful eyes, that have not seen
   The promised loveliness : for changeful Spring
   Has quickly passed, and summer does but bring
Scorched buds and flowers, that tell what might have
     been.

The trees are dark against the tender blue ;
   A deeper shade has bronzed the purple beech,
But even yet, the red leaves bud anew :
And thus, 'mid barren splendours of July,
   Fresh, brilliant hopes burst forth in glowing speech,
And light some pensive heart, before they die.

SUNSET.

The sun is setting—not in colours gay,
    But pure as when he blazed with noonday heat;
    The upland path is gold before my feet,
Save where long, dancing, poplar-shadows play,
Or arching lindens cast a broader gray:
    This radiant hour, when peace and passion meet,
    Stirs with tumultuous breezes, freshly sweet,
The odorous languor of an August day.

Above is peace; below is gleeful strife;
    Aflame with sunshine, battling with the wind,
The trees rejoice in plenitude of life:
A sea of light is sleeping in the west,
    Untroubled light, o'erflowing heart and mind
With that empyreal rapture, which is rest.

SEPTEMBER, 1880.

To still September comes a dream of joy:
   The breath of dying roses in the calm
   And sultry air, seems changed to hyacinth-balm;
Fresh beams and breezes waken, such as toy
With amorous wind-flowers and May-lilies coy:
   Raise, oh ye birds, a wild conjubilant psalm!
   Autumn has reached the goal, has gained the palm,
And Winter comes not surely to destroy.

Nay, prosperous Autumn! not for thee shall ope
   May's blossoms; nor for thy dull ear shall sing
Her choir of birds; thine own winds whirl away
Thy golden vapours, and thy rich decay,
   Till Winter come, stern pioneer of Spring,
Renewing Earth by terror and by hope.

SONGS BEFORE DAYBREAK.

The birds are singing, though it is not morn,
    Though in the east no rays of glory shine :
    Made clear by hope, their eyes and hearts divine
That in the dusky twilight, day is born.
Trusting they carol, though the heavens warn
    Their fearless joy with many a threatening sign;
    Though, still untinged with gold, the clouds combine,
While moans the rain-fraught wind, a voice forlorn.

Yes, wake me with your warbling, happy birds,
    That I may feel, before I see, the day;
That I may muse of hope, while in my heart
The notes translate themselves in gladsome words :
    E'en plashing rain-drops mingle with your lay,
And in its harmony the wind has part.

THE SEED.

No light of sun or moon can reach the seed
    That blindly in the bosom of a flower
    Ripens through summer, till its living power
Breaks the frail clasp that held it, and is freed :
Yet not with new-found sunshine can it feed
    The embryo life, that lighted but an hour
    Waits long in utter night its glorious dower :
Cold grows the earth, and spring time shall not speed.

Not as when warm in fragrant gloom it lay,
    But living hopeless, tombed in frost-bound sod,
    Now seems it poorer than the lifeless clod,
That lies above it, open to the day :
    Yet Night shall keep her own, and lose not one,
    And every child of Day shall find the sun.

OCTOBER, 1879.

Through all the dolorous year mine eyes have sought
    The ever-living loveliness that cleaves
    Even to dim grey skies and rain-bent sheaves;
Still is my garden with such beauty fraught,
And bright azaleas flash me back my thought;
    Their sunny flowers are fallen, but the leaves
    Flame gold and scarlet, and my heart receives
Delight more full than spring or summer brought.

And I can twine a rich October crown
    With branchlets of the golden-tressëd birch,
Green cedar plumes, and beech-leaves ruddy brown,
And woodbine gems, of pure translucent red;
    Even some lonely flowers may cheer my search,
Sweet as new joys that spring when hope is dead.

NOVEMBER, 1878.

The sky is dim and silent; lost are mirth,
    Colour, and motion; e'en the winds are dumb,
    Save for a constant, faint, unchanging hum,
That seems the voice of the despairing earth.
The birds are pining in this wintry dearth;
    The trees, that rang with carols frolicsome,
    Show dead black branches, fringed with white, whence come
No whispered hopes of any future birth.

And yet to me, the season still is fair,
    Though things of joy so sad and cold become:
Majestic stand the trunks and branches bare,
Their lace-like twigs half-seen, half-hid with snow:
    One frost-bit flower, a red chrysanthemum
Tells of the hidden store of life below.

DECEMBER, 1879.

Now is the Earth at rest from sun and storm;
   And stripped of all her gems and vestures gay,
   Gives thanks to Heaven, while weaklings can but pray:
In germs of life, uncouth of hue and form,
She feels the glory of the summer swarm,
   And knows December not less rich than May;
   For she is young as on her primal day,
And still beneath the snow her heart is warm.

All flowers and fruits are folded in her breast,
   Waiting but fuller radiance from above;
   And she lies dreaming of her destined hour,
All white and still, most like a soul at rest,
   Rich in hid wealth, and strong in secret power,
Silent with joy, and pure with perfect love.

UNDISCERNED PERFECTION.

BEYOND the realm of dull and slumberous Night
    I long have wandered with unwearied feet;
    The land where Poetry and Science meet
Streaks the far distance with a magic light:
Fair visions glide before my dazzled sight,
    And shine, and change, and pass with motion fleet,
    But never clear, and steadfast, and complete
In one transcendent brilliancy unite.

I know, the seeming discord is but mine;
    The glory is too great for mortal eyes,
All powerless to discover the divine
    And perfect harmony of earth and skies:
I know that each confused and tortuous line,
    To fuller sight, in true perspective lies.

THE PAINTER TO THE MUSICIAN.

Oh, sing once more, nor think your subtle spells
   Are vainly woven for a nature cold,
   Although I kneel not at the shrine of gold
Wherein the spirit of your worship dwells :
For when your voice in tones impassioned swells,
   The hosts of Dreamland are by you controlled,
   And secrets higher than my words unfold
Even to me the perfect music tells.

And your devotion is akin to mine,
   Though I give praise in colour, you in song ;
The self-same goddess, in another shrine,
   Counts me among the servitors who throng
Her outer courts : to Poesy divine
   Our noblest work, our deepest thoughts, belong.

SPEECH AND SILENCE.

When some sweet voice flows forth in foreign speech,
   The soul shines through the words, and makes
      them clear,
And all we see interprets all we hear,
For smiles and frowns have wondrous power to teach:
And voiceless grief our inmost heart can reach,
   With calm, deep gaze, too sad for hope or fear:
   Our eyes are wet for those who shed no tear,
And lips that Death has silenced, yet may preach.

In stillness we must win our deepest lore,
   Or 'mid the speechless chant of earth and sea:
Truth is a spirit, bodiless and free;
Imaged in words, 'tis perfect truth no more,
   For all our lofty visions fade and flee,
And song begins, when ecstasy is o'er.

BEAUTY.

ETERNAL Beauty, Truth's interpreter,
   Is bound by no austere æsthetic creed;
   All forms of art she uses at her need,
And e'en unlovely things are slaves to her:
And we, whose hearts her lightest breath can stir,
   Must prize her flowers, whoe'er has sown the seed,
   And love each noble picture, song, or deed,
Whose soul is true, although the form should err.

She is God's servant, but the queen of man,
   Who fondly dreams she lives for him alone,
   And while her power is felt through time and space,
Proclaims her priestess of some petty clan,
   Catching but transient glimpses of a face
Veiled in rich vestures, loved but still unknown.

THE MYSTERY OF LIGHT.

Light, glorious and eternal, that reveals
 All earthly things, itself is secret still;
 Love, silent king of heart, and mind, and will,
In lustrous mystery his power conceals;
And many a clouded spirit dumbly feels,
 But knows not, sees not yet, those truths that fill
 With beauty and with joy the dwellings chill
Even of Life that wounds, of Death that heals.

Yet Light, and Love, and Truth are all our own,
 And minister to us, who know them not;
  Fair hopes, that look like memories, will throng
E'en hearts that live in darkness and alone,
  And seem to chant some half-remembered song,
 The notes recalled, the lovely words forgot.

ILLUSIONS.

Not in the heavens alone is Truth renowned;
  Sad human hearts, that seem to love her less,
  Even in mutiny her power confess:
We speak in fables, and are compassed round
With poesy, distilling song from sound,
  Colour from light, and hope from happiness;
  Subliming weakness, yearning, and distress,
To that high faith, wherewith our life is crowned.

All fair deceits are prophets of the truth,
  E'en as the desert mirage tells a tale
    Of palms and wells, real, though far away:
The star-bright hopes that light the world's dim youth
  Are not too brilliant, but too silvery pale,
    To sparkle still, when dawns the golden day.

DAY-DREAMS.

Full oft through some enchanted land I tread,
  Wherein can live no hatred, pain, or fear,
  Where all the heavens with Truth's own light are
      clear,
And Love's own tints o'er all the earth are spread;
Where, through illumined foliage overhead,
  Swift, bright-winged birds will flash and disappear,
  While murmuring voices from the leaves I hear,
Repeating all my heart in secret said.

Not there I dwell, and yet my home is there;
  Those flower-grown paths I trod, a lonely child,
Breathing with simple joy the fragrant air:
Lured on by half-seen beauty even then,
With restless feet I roamed from hill to glen,
  By gleaming birds, by whispering leaves beguiled.

MORNING TWILIGHT.

There is a time, when all the heart is dumb,
   Too tired for dread of ill, or hope of good;
   When o'er dull brain and heavy eyelids brood
Shades of dead grief, endured and overcome,
Whose ghostly presence lingering doth benumb
   The constant soul, that gazed with hardihood
   On living evil: in this twilight mood
Even the sun and wind are wearisome.

Yet is their flickering strife but joy begun;
   For e'en the spectral shades grow faintly bright,
Like night-born mist, half kindled by the sun:
   Then shut not out the breeze, nor bar the light;
Full noon shall glow for him, who will not shun
   Heaven's dazzling joy-break, though tears cloud his
      sight.

SEMELE.

For her who loves a God, all hope must die
   Of sweet familiar joys, that daily move
   A woman's soul; of gentle cares, that prove
Her free devotion; of the answering eye,
Where speaks the heart, and hears each mute reply:
   Yes, these and more she lacks; yet far above
   That earthly home, expands her heaven of love,
And he she worships glows in sea and sky.

She whom the Sun has wooed—for whom his rays
   Have shone but once, unclouded—well may wait
   Through blackest night; her hope is one with fate:
Let me behold thee, Zeus! Dispel the haze
   That shields too tenderly my mortal sight:
   If life be darkness, let it cease in light.

THE PRIEST'S PRAYER.

HAVE pity, Lord! Let me not die alone!
   Though once I dared my fellow-souls to shrive,
   I am unclean; with pangs of death I strive.
Alas, what healing balm to me was known
For every heart that made its fevered moan!
   But now that *I* am sick, who shall revive
   My hopeless faith, or save my soul alive,
Since that elixir fails, which was mine own?

Spirit of God, Who dwellest e'en in me,
   Who speakest even by this doubtful breath,
Whether for good or ill Thou set me free,
   Withhold not Truth, although its price be Death:
I faint, I die, in scorching plains accurst,
Let me drink hemlock, if it slake my thirst!

WEARINESS.

TELL me no more, I must not fear to die;
   Ye waste your words; not death, but life I dread:
   Oh, to be numbered with the tranquil dead!
For I am tired; I do but crave to lie
Under the turf; only for rest I cry;
   And yet ye bid me turn my weary head,
   And on the scroll that hangs beside my bed
Read of another life, a home on high.

'Tis strange to think I once had power to cope
   With those who hate the Christ, and scorn His word;
   Sore were my wounds; my triumphs, oh, how few!
But now, at last, my prayer for sleep is heard:
   Forgive me, Lord! Thy promises are true,
And yet I have not strength enough to hope.

THE AGNOSTIC'S PSALM.

OH Thou, who art the life of heaven and earth,
    Eternal Substance of all things that seem ;
    Or but the glorious phantom of a dream
That in the brain of mortal man has birth :
To know that Thou dost live were little worth,
    Not knowing Thee ; yet oft the heart will deem
    That through its inmost deeps Thy light doth stream,
Bestowing peace for grief, calm joy for mirth.

E'en thus rich music enters tuneless ears,
    Tuneless, and all untrained by ordered notes,
    Yet its ethereal essence inward floats,
And mingling with the secret source of tears,
    Awhile endues the spirit's wistful sight
    With dim perceptions of unknown delight.

TO AMY, ON RECEIVING HER PHOTOGRAPH.

When of some lovely landscape unforgot
    A shadowy sketch I see, my thought divines
    Clear sunshine gleaming through the pencilled lines,
And cool green shade, where seems a shapeless blot :
I know how morning pierced that sheltered grot,
    How noonday glowed between the tufted pines ;
    And even so, your cold grey portrait shines
With tints unseen by those who know you not.

They cannot see the apple-blossom cheek,
    The eyes of midnight blue, the sun-lit hair ;
Grave are the lips, and will not smile or speak ;
    And yet to me the pictured face is fair :
I conned that May-tide bloom when last we met,
And all the eye saw then, the heart sees yet.

STARLIGHT. I.

Night works like Time : hushed is the busy street ;
   Grey are the walls, whose yet untarnished red
   Glared in the sun ; for shadows overspread
All hues of earth, that wearied eyes may meet
The restful heavens ; that mortal hearts may greet
   Eternal truth : while darksome paths I tread,
   The light of other worlds is round me shed,
The glow of distant æons guides my feet.

The silent stars my ecstasy control ;
   No daring hopes, no awe-struck fears intrude
Upon the calm rejoicing of the soul :
From sun to sun, from age to age I climb,
   Until for Space I see Infinitude,
And feel Eternity, where was but Time.

STARLIGHT. II.

Man needs no dread unwonted Avatar
    The secrets of the heavenly host to show;
    From waves of light, their lustrous founts we know,
For every gleaming band and shadowed bar
Is fraught with homelike tidings from afar;
    Each ripple, starting long decades ago,
    Pulsing to earth its blue or golden glow,
Beats with the life of some immortal star.

A life to each minutest atom given—
    Whether it find in Man's own heart a place,
    Or past the suns, in unimagined space—
That Earth may know herself a part of Heaven,
    And see, wherever sun or spark is lit,
    One Law, one Life, one Substance infinite.

TRANSLATIONS.

THE KNIGHT OF TOGGENBURG.

From the German of Schiller.

" KNIGHT, with sister's love for brother,
    Dear to me thou art:
Take this love, and ask no other,
    For it grieves my heart:
Calmly coming, calmly going,
    Welcome shouldst thou be,
But these tears, in silence flowing,
    These are strange to me."

To his bosom, dumbly aching,
    Wild the maid he wrings,
Then away in anguish breaking
    On his charger springs;

From their mountains, where they tarry,
 Calls his Switzers brave;
On their breast the Cross they carry
 To the Holy Grave.

Wondrous deeds that host undaunted
 Have in fight performed,
Every helmet's plume has flaunted
 Where the foemen swarmed;
Toggenburg, that name victorious,
 Frights the Moslem train,
But his heart, 'mid triumphs glorious,
 Is not healed from pain.

He has borne a year of sorrow,
 Now can bear no more,
Wins no respite, night or morrow,
 Rides from camp to shore;
Sees a ship, with canvas flying,
 Joppa's haven leaves,
Home to that dear country hieing
 Where her bosom heaves.

Now the pilgrim nears her castle,
    Now his knock is heard;
Woe! 'tis opened by a vassal
    With the thunder-word—
"She you seek, to God is given,
    Veiled before Him bows,
Yestermorn, the bride of Heaven
    Sealed her marriage vows."

Now his father's castle never
    Shall receive its lord,
Faithful steed he leaves for ever,
    Helm, and lance, and sword;
From the Toggenburg down-stealing,
    Tells to none his name,
'Neath a gown of hair concealing
    His majestic frame.

And a little hut he raises
    Looking towards the glade
Where the convent darkly gazes
    From the linden shade:

Waiting from the morn's first blushing
    Till the sunset shone,
Silent hope his features flushing,
    Sat he there alone,

Towards the convent gazing, yearning,
    Kept for hours his watch,
To his loved one's window turning.
    Till she clinked the latch,
Till the face and form entrancing
    From the window smiled,
Downward o'er the valley glancing,
    Peaceful, angel-mild.

Now rejoicing, healed from sadness,
    Down to sleep he lay,
Woke again with quiet gladness
    At the dawn of day:
So he sat for many a morrow,
    Kept for years his watch,
Waiting mutely, void of sorrow,
    Till she clinked the latch,

Till the face and form entrancing
    From the window smiled,
Downward o'er the valley glancing,
    Peaceful, angel-mild.
So he sat, when morning's brightness
    Dead and cold he met,
With a face of placid whiteness,
    Towards her window set.

THE MAIDEN'S LAMENT.

From the German of Schiller.

THE oak-wood murmurs,
  The sky clouds o'er,
The maiden paces
  The grassy shore;
The billows are breaking with might, with might,
And she sighs aloud in the gloomy night;
  Her eyes all heavy with sadness:

"The heart is broken,
  The world is void,
With empty pleasures
  My soul is cloyed;
Thou Holy One, summon thy child above;
I have lived my life, I have loved my love,
  And revelled in earthly gladness."

"The tears that thou weepest
All vainly are shed,
No power hath thy plaining
To waken the dead;
But tell me, what comforts and gladdens the heart
When the joys of sweet Love must for ever depart;
I, the Holy One, bend to thy crying."

"Let the tears I am weeping
All vainly be shed,
Let my plaining be powerless
To waken the dead:
The sweetest delight for the sorrowful heart
When the joys of bright Love must for ever depart,
Is Love's own weeping and sighing."

THE SHARING OF EARTH.

From the German of Schiller.

"Take ye the world," cried Zeus from Heaven's
    height,
  "Ye sons of men! I give it all to you,
A heritage in everlasting right;
    Now share the gift, as brethren do."

Then hasted every hand to grasp its gain,
    And young or old, each claimed his share of good;
Soon clutched the Husbandman his golden grain;
    The Squire rode hunting through the wood;

The Merchant bustled, till his wares were stowed;
    The Abbot chose him generous cobwebbed wine;
The Monarch barred the river and the road,
    Crying "The tenth of all is mine."

THE SHARING OF EARTH.

Late, when the last had long received his share,
    The Poet came, from regions far and dim;
Too late! each heritage had found an heir,
    And nought, alas! was left for him.

"Ah, woe is me! Of all thy sons, shall I,
    The truest, be forgotten? I alone?"
Loud to the ears of Zeus he sent his cry,
    And threw himself before the throne.

"Nay, if in dreamland thou wert pleased to hide,"
    Rejoined the God, "accuse thyself, not me;
Where, while they portioned Earth, didst *thou* abide?"
    "I was," the Poet said, "with thee.

"Mine eye was fixed on thy celestial face,
    Mine ear upon the harmonies of Heaven;
If, by thy light entranced, I lost my place
    On Earth, oh, be the fault forgiven!"

"What help?" said Zeus: "the Earth is given away,
    Mart, greenwood, harvest, these no more are mine;
But, if thou be content with *me* to stay,
    Come when thou wilt, a home in Heaven is thine!"

COMFORT IN TEARS.

From the German of Goethe.

Why art thou sad, when all around
   So gay and bright appears?
For plainly in thine eyes are seen
   The traces of thy tears.

" And if I wept in solitude
   The grief is mine alone,
And with the tears that sweetly streamed,
   More light my heart has grown."

Come, let us clasp thee in our arms,
   Thy joyous comrades say;
And there, whatever thou hast lost,
   Weep thy regrets away.

" Ye brawl and bluster, dreaming not
   The secret of my pain;
My grief is not that I have lost,
   But that I long in vain."

Spring boldly up; for thou art young,
   With speed thy task begin;
Thine is the age of daring deeds,
   And strength to strive and win.

" Ah no ! 'tis what I cannot win,
   From me 'tis all too far;
It dwells as high, it gleams as bright,
   As shineth yonder star."

We do not long to reach the stars
   But glory in their light,
And gaze to heaven in ecstasy
   Each fair and cloudless night.

" I, too, look up in ecstasy,
   By day my watch I keep,
Then let me weep the nights away
   While I have heart to weep."

THE WANDERER'S NIGHT-SONG.

From the German of Goethe.

Thou, who Heaven's angel art,
   Thou, who pain and sorrow stillest,
And the doubly mournful heart
   With a double comfort fillest!
Ah, what weary days I number!
Why this sad or gay unrest?
   Sweetest slumber
Come, oh come, to calm my breast!

EVENING.

From the German of Goethe.

O'er every mountain height
 Slumber broods,
Scarcely a zephyr light
 Stirs in the woods
 One leafy crest;
The song-bird sleeps on the bough.
Wait a little, and thou,
 Thou too, shalt rest.

BURY THE DEAD THOU LOVEST.

From the German of Carl Siebel.

Bury the dead thou lovest,
    Deep, deep within thy heart;
So shall they live and love thee
    Till Life and thou shall part.

So for their risen spirits
    Thy breast a heaven shall be;
Like angels, pure and shining,
    They go through life with thee.

Bury the life thou livest
    Deep in another's heart;
So shalt thou live belovëd
    When dead and cold thou art.

SPRING.

From the German of Ernst Schulze.

Oh come, sweet Spring! thy budding flowers unfold;
   Within the woods awake the song-bird's lay,
   And gloriously adorn thy kingdom gay
With light, perfume, and clouds beflecked with gold.
All trees shall chant in Love's own murmurous tone,
   With Love the stream shall sing, the forest glow:
   My heart, perchance, that home of midnight woe,
Circled with joy, shall deem that joy its own.

Alas for me! Why sadly, mutely look
   After long-vanished beams, that once were bright?
   Why call in vain the ghosts of days more fair?
She who from out my life all gladness took,
   From Springtide, too, has stolen Love's delight,
   And nothing left, save only Love's despair.

THE RUINED MILL.

From the German of Julius Sturm.

The moon is newly risen,
   I wander through the vale;
My dreaming eyes are spell-bound
   By radiance sad and pale.

Behind the mill she rises;
   I watch her silver shield,
And in my heart burst open
   The wounds I thought were healed.

Long since, the wheels have mouldered,
   And roof and door are gone;
Babbling of days departed
   The glittering stream flows on.

The moon has sunk in darkness,
   The wind is blowing cold;
Dead is the miller's daughter,
   And I am grey and old.

THE FIR-TREE.

From the German of Luise von Ploennies.

HIGH on that hill thou seest
    A single fir-tree stand;
I sit there every morning,
    And gaze across the land.

The stork comes flying swiftly,
    The field with flowers is gay;
But into the world, my sweetheart
    Has travelled far away.

And roses bloom in the garden,
    And they cut the ripened grain;
And still I wait for my sweetheart,
    He yet may come again.

And the leaves have grown so golden,
    The leaves have grown so red;
And if my sweetheart will not come,
    I would that I were dead!

THE FIR-TREE.

Oh why hast thou, green fir-tree,
    No red and gold array?
Oh, fiery love within me,
    Why dost thou burn for aye?

Oh, fir-tree, dark-green fir-tree,
    Why art thou not sere and old
Oh, fiery heart within me,
    When, when wilt thou be cold?

THE WELL.

From the German of Paul Heyse.

Yes, wayward girl, be cold and shy,
    From morn till eve lock up thy heart;
The flashing lustre of thine eye
    Must still betray how rich thou art.

That legendary tale they tell
    Comes back, while thus I gaze and think:
In some old city lay a well,
    Whose virgin waters none might drink.

So deep, so fathomless a well,
    So wondrous deep, that when they let
A pitcher down, for hours it fell,
    And had not reached the bottom yet.

A minstrel, wandering through the land,
    Espied it, as he passed along;
He took his fiddle in his hand,
    And played a tune and sang a song.

And hark! a sound unwonted here,
   A rising, rushing, surging, splashing,
Of water sweet, and cool, and clear,
   High over the brim exuberant dashing.

The minstrel drank a joyous draught,
   And all the neighbours shared his glee:
What boundless bliss must he have quaffed,
   Whose voice could set the fountain free!

AN EVENING SONG.

From the German of Rückert.

I stood upon the mountain
    Before the sun had set,
And saw how o'er the forest
    Hung evening's golden net.

Earth was bedewed with slumber,
    Shed from the clouded sky,
And all the bells of even
    Sang Nature's lullaby.

I said—Oh heart, acknowledge
    The sleep of earth and air,
And with the meadow's children,
    Rest thou from all thy care.

For all the little blossoms
    Their eyelids gently close,
And with a softer motion
    The streamlet's current flows.

And now the sylph, grown weary,
    Under a leaf doth hide;
The dragon-fly, dew-sprinkled,
    Sleeps at the river-side.

Now in his rose-leaf cradle
    The golden beetle rocks;
Back to the fold are hasting
    The shepherd and his flocks.

The lark flies earthward, seeking
    His clover-shaded nest,
And in the wood's recesses
    Lie hart and doe at rest.

And he who has a cottage
    There to his rest has lain,
And he who lives in exile,
    In dreams goes home again.

An eager yearning fills me:
    In vain I long to climb
Up to my own true country
    By mountain paths of time.

MY ONLY ONE.

From the German of J. G. Fischer.

Thou knowest well, that thou art all I have;
  Oh, do not turn thy lovely eyes from me,
  When of the joys of love I speak to thee;
    For thou art all I have.

Thou knowest well, that thou art all I have;
  Why wilt thou envying on the blossoms look,
  Withered too soon, and drifting down the brook?
    Since thou art all I have.

Thou knowest well, that thou art all I have;
  But oh, I feel that thou wilt soon depart,
  And leave in loneliness this mournful heart;
    Though thou art all I have.

FAREWELL.

From the German of Emmanuel Geibel.

One goblet more I drink to thee,
    Thou fair and foreign strand;
No sadder could this parting be
    Wert thou my native land.

Farewell, farewell! The sails are spread,
    The wind blows fresh and free;
Its trail of foam the keel has led
    Along the deep-green sea.

Now sinks the sun 'mid islets fair,
    And rose-red shines the sky;
'Twas in the hut that glimmers there
    We said our last good-bye.

And oh! how gladly would I stay,
    Thou lovely child, with thee!
In vain! the vision fades away
    That was so fair to see.

For this is life—to come, to go,
    To haste o'er sea and shore,
The joys of rest awhile to know,
    Then part for ever more.

Loved for a time, forgotten quite,
    But mutely loving yet—
Is it the dazzling sunset light
    That makes my eyes so wet?

'Tis past! I dash the tear away,
    And joy with grief has flown;
This restless heart, where'er I stray,
    Must beat henceforth alone.

Well, be it so! Far o'er the main
    The moon's first ray is bright;
The coast recedes—Yet once again,
    My little maid, good-night!

www.ingramcontent.com/pod-product-compliance
Lightning Source LLC
Chambersburg PA
CBHW020248170426
43202CB00008B/282